First Ladies

Harriet Lane

Jill C. Wheeler

ABDO
Publishing Company

visit us at
www.abdopublishing.com

Published by ABDO Publishing Company, 8000 West 78th Street, Edina, Minnesota 55439.
Copyright © 2010 by Abdo Consulting Group, Inc. International copyrights reserved in all
countries. No part of this book may be reproduced in any form without written permission from the
publisher. The Checkerboard Library™ is a trademark and logo of ABDO Publishing Company.

Printed in the United States.

Manufactured with paper containing at least 10% post-consumer waste

Cover Photo: iStockphoto
Interior Photos: Alamy pp. 11, 24; AP Images p. 13; Art Resource pp. 19, 26; Corbis p. 7;
    Getty Images p. 18; The Granger Collection pp. 5, 15; iStockphoto p. 21;
    Library of Congress p. 23; North Wind pp. 9, 16; Picture History p. 22

Series Coordinator: BreAnn Rumsch
Editors: Heidi M.D. Elston, BreAnn Rumsch
Art Direction & Cover Design: Neil Klinepier

Library of Congress Cataloging-in-Publication Data

Wheeler, Jill C., 1964-
  Harriet Lane / Jill C. Wheeler.
     p. cm. -- (First ladies)
  ISBN 978-1-60453-631-7
  1. Johnston, Harriet Lane, 1830-1903--Juvenile literature. 2. Buchanan, James, 1791-1868--
Family--Juvenile literature. 3. Presidents--United States--Family--Juvenile literature. I. Title.

  E437.1.W47 2010
  973.6'8092--dc22
  [B]
                                        2009009988

Contents

Harriet Lane

Harriet Lane acted as First Lady from 1857 to 1861. Unlike other First Ladies, she was not married to the president. Instead, she served as White House hostess for her **bachelor** uncle James Buchanan. He was the fifteenth president of the United States.

Miss Lane fulfilled many of the First Lady's duties. She lived at the White House and managed the household. And as White House hostess, Miss Lane received and entertained the president's guests.

President Buchanan was not the first president to have a White House hostess. The wives of several presidents died before their husbands took office. These presidents include Thomas Jefferson and Martin Van Buren. In place of their wives, White House hostesses managed social events.

Miss Lane was just 26 when she took on the duties of First Lady. Though she was young, she was calm and charming. Her elegance and personality captivated the nation. Miss Lane was a role model for Americans, too. She often worked to help others. For these reasons, Miss Lane has been called the first modern First Lady.

Harriet Lane is unique among First Ladies. She carried out her role under the nation's only bachelor president.

Orphaned

Harriet Rebecca Lane was born on May 9, 1830, in Mercersburg, Pennsylvania. She was the youngest child of Elliott and Jane Buchanan Lane. Elliott was a successful merchant. Jane cared for their home and four children.

As a young girl, Harriet was cheerful and outgoing. She was also competitive and athletic. She preferred climbing trees to sitting quietly and reading books.

Early on, Harriet's world changed greatly. When she was just nine years old, her mother died. Her father died two years later. At age 11, Harriet was an orphan.

Harriet had always been especially fond of her uncle James Buchanan. So in 1841, she requested he take her in. When Mr. Buchanan learned Harriet wanted him to become her guardian, he quickly agreed. He looked forward to bringing up his "mischievous romp of a niece."

At the time, Mr. Buchanan was a U.S. senator. He had begun his career as a lawyer in Lancaster, Pennsylvania. Then, he built a successful career in politics.

Harriet and her uncle got along well. Every day, they discussed literature and the news. Harriet showed an interest in politics. So, Mr. Buchanan allowed her to attend his political meetings. She amused him by imitating the politicians.

Mr. Buchanan encouraged Harriet's intelligence. He gave her full access to his library.

A Spirited Girl

Until 1844, Harriet was educated in Pennsylvania. Then, Mr. Buchanan sent her to Charlestown, West Virginia. There, she attended boarding school for three years. While Harriet was away, her uncle wrote to her often.

Harriet spent her school vacations with her uncle. They often stayed in Washington, D.C. Sometimes during the summers, they traveled to Bedford Springs, Pennsylvania. Harriet liked her new life. Her uncle let her do almost anything she wanted.

Eventually, Mr. Buchanan received a letter from her school's director. The woman suggested that Harriet stop spending school vacations in Washington. She warned that Harriet would grow up spoiled.

Mr. Buchanan decided it was time for a change. So in 1847, Harriet entered the Academy of the Visitation Convent in Washington, D.C. Many prominent families sent their daughters to this academy. There, young ladies learned how to behave in society.

Harriet called her uncle "Nunc," and he called her "Hal."

8

Young Socialite

For the next two years, Harriet thrived at her new school. She enjoyed studying history, astronomy, mythology, and art. Harriet soon became a skilled dancer and musician. She especially enjoyed playing the piano.

Harriet quickly became a popular member of Washington society, too. Many young men wanted to date her. Harriet called her suitors pleasant but troublesome.

Harriet's uncle cautioned her about marrying too quickly. Instead, he urged her to take her time and choose wisely. Harriet decided to follow her uncle's advice.

In 1849, Harriet graduated from the Academy of the Visitation Convent. She then moved to Wheatland, her uncle's new estate near Lancaster. There, Harriet devoted herself to acting as his hostess.

Harriet was a natural hostess. She loved dancing, music, and meeting people. Harriet was never shy about making new friends. Later, this skill would come in very handy.

In addition to hostessing, Harriet was responsible for decorating and furnishing Wheatland.

A Quiet Campaign

Meanwhile, Mr. Buchanan had worked to advance his political career. Miss Lane knew how much her uncle wanted to be elected U.S. president. Twice, he had failed to win the **Democratic** Party's presidential nomination. Then in 1848, Mr. Buchanan had retired from public service.

But in 1851, Pennsylvania Democrats urged Mr. Buchanan to run for president again. Miss Lane hoped to help her uncle succeed. Yet at that time, it was not suitable for women to campaign.

Miss Lane did not let that stop her. That winter, she quietly met with a Pennsylvania mayor named David Lynch. Lynch was an important Democratic leader. He recognized that Miss Lane understood politics well. So, he listened to what she had to say. After this, Miss Lane was well respected by many politicians.

Mr. Buchanan did not win the 1852 nomination. Instead, Democrat Franklin Pierce became president in 1853. That year, he named Mr. Buchanan minister to England. Mr. Buchanan's post would take him to London. Miss Lane was thrilled with her uncle's new job. She asked to go with him and act as his hostess. Mr. Buchanan granted her wish.

Harriet was a beautiful girl with violet eyes and blonde hair.

Life in London

Miss Lane arrived in England in April 1854. Soon after, she was introduced to the royal **court**. For the meeting, Miss Lane wore an impressive gown. The train alone was made from 100 yards (91 m) of white lace! She also wore diamonds and ostrich feathers on her head.

Court visitors were expected to show respect for the royal family. Miss Lane behaved perfectly. She especially impressed Queen Victoria. The queen granted Miss Lane the rank of an ambassador's wife. This was a very special honor.

During her time in London, Miss Lane charmed the entire royal family. Her knowledge of politics and literature impressed them. So did her skilled horsemanship. Miss Lane became a favorite of the queen. She got along well with other members of the court, too.

Miss Lane loved her time in England. She enjoyed English people and **customs**. Yet, she never forgot her own background. Miss Lane often used social occasions to present the American point of view.

Victoria became queen
in 1837, when she was
just 18 years old.

The Democratic Queen

Miss Lane returned to the United States with her uncle in 1855. At that time, slavery threatened peace in the country. Southern states believed slavery should be legal. Northern states argued that slavery was wrong.

That year, the **Democratic** Party nominated Mr. Buchanan for U.S. president. He won the election the next year! He took office in March 1857. President Buchanan had never married. So, he asked his niece to serve as the First Lady. Miss Lane happily accepted this role. As First Lady, she would act as the official White House hostess.

It wasn't long before Miss Lane became a popular First Lady and trendsetter. She loved to wear beautiful gowns. She lowered the neckline of these dresses. Soon, women around the country were copying her fashions and her hairstyles.

Miss Lane also made the capital city more stylish. She filled the White House with music and flowers. And, she held elegant parties. While in London, Miss Lane had developed a great love of art. As First Lady, she often invited artists and musicians to White House events.

The First Lady's attitude and hostessing skills were unexpected in someone so young. Her popularity led some people to call her the Democratic Queen. Songs, dances, and ships were named in her honor.

Both President Buchanan and Miss Lane loved to entertain. After her uncle took office, Miss Lane hosted a ball for 6,000 guests!

Gracious First Lady

Albert, Prince of Wales, went on to become the king of England.

Every morning, Miss Lane and President Buchanan read the newspapers together. They discussed the challenges facing the nation. Like many First Ladies, Miss Lane spoke with the president on a regular basis. So, people often sought access to him through her. She was happy to help whenever she could.

As a student, Miss Lane had been encouraged to help others. She never forgot this lesson. As First Lady, she promoted better education, new hospitals, and prison reform.

The First Lady also spoke out for improved treatment of Native

*Miss Lane, Prince Albert, President Buchanan, and others traveled to
Mount Vernon aboard a ship named* Harriet Lane.

Americans. Her support earned her the name "Great Mother of the
Indians." In addition, many Native Americans named their
daughters after her.

In 1860, the First Lady repaid England's royal family for their
earlier generosity. Albert, Prince of Wales, came to visit the United
States. Miss Lane welcomed him with a grand state dinner at the
White House.

The First Lady kept the prince entertained. She arranged a visit
to former president George Washington's home, Mount Vernon. She
also held a bowling match for the prince. The First Lady even beat
him at the game! Prince Albert thoroughly enjoyed his stay. His visit
was a highlight of President Buchanan's term.

Road to War

During President Buchanan's four years in the White House, political opposition grew. Arguments between Northerners and Southerners continued to break out.

In the White House, Miss Lane did her best to limit these conflicts. She carefully seated known opponents away from each other at dinner parties. And, she did not allow guests to discuss politics at dinner.

As First Lady, Miss Lane demonstrated much grace dealing with others. Yet, she and President Buchanan could not solve the nation's problems. Before his term ended, seven Southern states **seceded** from the **Union**. Some people blamed the president. But, Miss Lane defended her uncle whenever she could.

President Buchanan had not won reelection in 1860. So in March 1861, he retired to Wheatland. Miss Lane went with him. The American **Civil War** began the next month. Miss Lane and her uncle lived quietly in Pennsylvania as the war raged on.

As First Lady, Miss Lane held large dinner parties every week. Usually, about 40 guests attended.

Love and Loss

The pressure of the past few years had worn on Mr. Buchanan. His health was failing. As Miss Lane cared for her uncle, she began thinking about her future. She had put off marriage for many years.

Then in October 1864, Miss Lane announced she was engaged to Henry Elliott Johnston. He was a banker from Baltimore, Maryland. Miss Lane and Henry had met in Bedford Springs in

Miss Lane on her wedding day

summer 1849. Henry had been interested in Miss Lane since that first meeting.

On January 11, 1866, the two were married at Wheatland. They traveled to Cuba for their **honeymoon**. Then, the Johnstons settled into a quiet life in Baltimore. They enjoyed a loving marriage.

The Johnstons happily welcomed two sons into their lives. James Buchanan was born in 1867. Henry Elliott Jr. was born two years later.

Upon his death, Mr. Buchanan left Wheatland to Miss Lane. She spent her summers there until she sold the estate.

Unfortunately, Mrs. Johnston also faced much sadness. Her favorite uncle, James Buchanan, had died in 1868. Then, both of Mr. and Mrs. Johnston's sons passed away as teenagers. James died of **rheumatic fever** in 1881. Henry died of the same disease the following year.

Gifts for the Nation

Johns Hopkins Hospital in Baltimore, Maryland

After losing her sons, Mrs. Johnston wanted to help other sick children. In 1883, she and her husband funded and began planning a project. It was called the Harriet Lane Home for Invalid Children. Mrs. Johnston wanted the home to be for children needing medical care.

Sadly, Mrs. Johnston's losses were not over. Mr. Johnston became ill and died on May 5, 1884. Mrs. Johnston was now alone once again. She decided to sell Wheatland and her Baltimore home. Then, she returned to Washington, D.C. Mrs. Johnston was happy to be back among her friends.

By this time, Mrs. Johnston was quite wealthy. She had received much money after the deaths of her uncle and her husband. This gave Mrs. Johnston the resources to support projects and organizations dear to her.

Mrs. Johnston worked to find the right organization to run the Harriet Lane Home. She decided she wanted the funds for it to go to Johns Hopkins Hospital after her death. Today, the home is part of the Johns Hopkins Children's Center.

The Harriet Lane Home

Harriet Lane cared deeply about helping needy children. So, she planned a home for them. She later gave funds to open the home at Johns Hopkins Hospital. With the hospital's help, the Harriet Lane Home for Invalid Children opened in 1912. It became the nation's first hospital for children.

Today, the home is known as the Harriet Lane Clinic. It serves as a top training site for medical students. Miss Lane instructed that the home should help all children. As a result, the clinic provides quality medical care to thousands each year.

Mrs. Johnston also continued traveling and collecting art. She added many new pieces to her personal collection. But by 1903, Mrs. Johnston's health was failing. That summer, she traveled to Narragansett, Rhode Island. There on July 3, she died from **cancer**. Mrs. Johnston was buried at Greenmount Cemetery in Baltimore. By the time of her death, Mrs. Johnston had acquired a sizable art collection.

Harriet Lane was one of the best-loved First Ladies in U.S. history.

Her **will** stated that it should be given to the federal government. However, there was one condition. The government could have the artwork only if a national gallery was formed.

Back in 1846, Congress had established the Smithsonian Institution in Washington, D.C. At that time, Congress stated the Smithsonian would include a national gallery. But when Mrs. Johnston died, the Smithsonian did not yet contain artwork.

Then in 1906, the U.S. **Supreme Court** declared the Smithsonian had a national gallery. Mrs. Johnston's art collection was one of the first to be **donated** to the Smithsonian. Her gift inspired other collectors to donate their art, too. Eventually, the Smithsonian's American Art Museum acquired Mrs. Johnston's collection.

In her will, Mrs. Johnston also gave money to found a school for choirboys. The school was called the National Cathedral School for Boys. It opened in Washington, D.C., in 1909. It was later renamed Saint Albans School.

Harriet Lane was a charming and intelligent First Lady. From her position as White House hostess, she brought elegance and style to Washington, D.C. Miss Lane also set an example for the nation. She inspired others to contribute to worthy projects. Today, her **legacy** lives on in her generous gifts.

Timeline

1830	On May 9, Harriet Rebecca Lane was born.
1841	Harriet went to live with her uncle James Buchanan.
1849	Harriet graduated from the Academy of the Visitation Convent; she began hostessing at Wheatland.
1854–1855	Miss Lane served as her uncle's hostess in England, while he was U.S. minister there.
1857–1861	Miss Lane acted as First Lady, while her uncle served as president.
1860	Miss Lane hosted Albert, Prince of Wales, at the White House.
1866	On January 11, Miss Lane married Henry Elliott Johnston.
1867	The Johnstons' son James Buchanan was born.
1868	Mrs. Johnston's uncle James Buchanan died.
1869	The Johnstons' son Henry Elliott Jr. was born.
1881	James died of rheumatic fever.
1882	Henry died of rheumatic fever.
1883	The Johnstons funded the Harriet Lane Home for Invalid Children.
1884	Mr. Johnston died on May 5.
1903	On July 3, Mrs. Johnston died.

Did You Know?

Harriet Lane is the only White House hostess to be called a First Lady.

Miss Lane is considered one of America's first serious art collectors. She was also one of the first to collect Native American artwork.

Miss Lane was the first First Lady to invite artists to the White House.

The Smithsonian Institution was grateful for Miss Lane's generous art donation. So, someone there once called her "First Lady of the National Collection of Fine Arts."

Miss Lane became the first White House resident to have a song dedicated to her. The song is called "Listen to the Mockingbird."

Three U.S. military ships have been named after Miss Lane. Today, the USCGC *Harriet Lane* is still in service under the U.S. Coast Guard.

In May 1860, Miss Lane hosted the first Japanese ambassadors to visit the United States.

Glossary

bachelor - a man who has not married.

cancer - any of a group of often deadly diseases marked by an abnormal growth of cells that destroys healthy tissues and organs.

civil war - a war between groups in the same country. The United States of America and the Confederate States of America fought a civil war from 1861 to 1865.

court - the family, the residence, the advisers, or the assemblies of a ruler.

custom - a habit of a group that is passed on through generations.

Democrat - a member of the Democratic political party. When James Buchanan was president, Democrats supported farmers and landowners.

donate - to give.

honeymoon - a trip or a vacation taken by a newly married couple.

legacy - something important or meaningful handed down from previous generations or from the past.

rheumatic fever (ru-MA-tihk FEE-vuhr) - a disease that occurs mainly in children. It is marked by fever and pain in the joints and especially in the lungs.

secede - to break away from a group.

Supreme Court - the highest, most powerful court in the United States.

Union - the states that remained in the United States during the Civil War.

will - a legal declaration of a person's wishes regarding the disposal of his or her property after death.

Web Sites

To learn more about Harriet Lane, visit ABDO Publishing Company on the World Wide Web at **www.abdopublishing.com**. Web sites about Harriet Lane are featured on our Book Links page. These links are routinely monitored and updated to provide the most current information available.

Index